To Isabella,

Enjoy!
Be Blessed!

Love,

A History Maker

My Life As A Victorious Overcomer

Laurie S. Ornstein

WestBow Press
A DIVISION OF THOMAS NELSON

Copyright © 2012 Laurie S. Ornstein.

All rights reserved. No part of this book may be used or reproduced by any means, graphic, electronic, or mechanical, including photocopying, recording, taping or by any information storage retrieval system without the written permission of the publisher except in the case of brief quotations embodied in critical articles and reviews.

ISBN: 978-1-4497-3780-1 (sc)
ISBN: 978-1-4497-3781-8 (e)
ISBN: 978-1-4497-3779-5 (hc)

Library of Congress Control Number: 2012900987

WestBow Press books may be ordered through booksellers or by contacting:

WestBow Press
A Division of Thomas Nelson
1663 Liberty Drive
Bloomington, IN 47403
www.westbowpress.com
1-(866) 928-1240

Because of the dynamic nature of the Internet, any web addresses or links contained in this book may have changed since publication and may no longer be valid. The views expressed in this work are solely those of the author and do not necessarily reflect the views of the publisher, and the publisher hereby disclaims any responsibility for them.

Any people depicted in stock imagery provided by Thinkstock are models, and such images are being used for illustrative purposes only.

Certain stock imagery © Thinkstock.

Printed in the United States of America

WestBow Press rev. date: 2/07/2012

Table of Contents

Acknowledgements vii
Forward xi
Introduction xiii

Chapter 1 1
Chapter 2 5
Chapter 3 7
Chapter 4 9
Chapter 5 11
Chapter 6 13
Chapter 7 17
Chapter 8 25
Chapter 9 29
Chapter 10 37
Chapter 11 39
Chapter 12 43
Chapter 13 47
Chapter 14 51
Chapter 15 53
Chapter 16 57

Chapter 17 59
Chapter 18 63
Chapter 19 67
Chapter 20 71
Chapter 21 79
Chapter 22 85
Chapter 23 87

Epilogue 89

Acknowledgements

First I would like to thank God the Father, Jesus, and The Holy Spirit; without whom I would not have been able to write this book.

A special thank you to Annie Seavers who encouraged and motivated me to write this book. Thank you Annie also for typing this manuscript. A special thank you also to Callie Becker who edited and re-edited this manuscript. I will be eternally grateful for the encouragement and support they have given me.

I would also like to thank my family, whom I love very much. They have encouraged me to write a book for over twenty years. Their love and support have been priceless.

Thank you to Samantha Tetro, who is a visionary, and opened up Samantha's Li'l Bit of Heaven Ministries. Her love and support during the past sixteen years have been extremely valuable. I would also like to thank Samantha for having had Pastor Karen Orlando and her family, along with Jeanine, Karen's right hand person, all of whom have ministered to us faithfully for the past seven years.

Thank you to Vincenzo Pasani, who has helped me walk every week for the past seven years. Without his help I wouldn't be walking nearly as well as I am today.

Thank you to all of the Pastors who have sown seeds into my life. I appreciate all of you.

Thank you to all of my brothers and sisters in the faith, my friends, and family, who I did not mention by name. You are nonetheless so important in my life with your support and encouragement.

Thank you to Anonymous, whose generous spirit helped make this dream a reality.

I would like to thank God for having blessed me with
Gertrude and Harvey Ornstein
the absolute best parents in the entire world

Forward

Laurie has a way of changing the vision of those around her just by living her life. She and I have gone to the same church for several years but I knew who she was long before we actually met. I would often see her gliding her electric wheelchair in all directions just in front of the altar as the music played during worship. Instead of standing up singing and clapping as many of us did, Laurie worshipped in the way that she was able. She guided that chair back and forth, turning and spinning as if dancing. Looking on, I could see that she gave it all that she had and her joy was obvious with each and every movement.

That's the kind of thing that sets Laurie apart. It's not the wheelchair, it's that passion. It's that spirit in her that gives everything she has to whatever she is doing. Some might feel sorry for her because of her limitations. But the truth is that Laurie is less limited than many people with fully functioning arms and legs. She doesn't seem bound by the limitations of a situation but instead sees the possibilities of it. And it's the same thing with people. She has to depend on others for most things but she is just focused on the needs of those around her as she is on her own.

In looking back I realize how Laurie, by example, has encouraged me when I felt inadequate or frustrated, humbled me when I became self-focused or impatient, and challenged me to live my life with purpose and meaning. I pray that you are blessed in reading her story as I have been in knowing her.

Joanne McCormack

Introduction

Lord Jesus, I love you so much for your goodness, mercy, and loving kindness. Today is November 16th, 2009...the day before my 46th birthday. For years, I have been longing and searching for a way to share with others the impact you have had on my life. There have been times when I was given the opportunity to reach out to others. On two separate occasions, Pastor Richard Anderson from the Holding Out Hope Church, in Middle Island, New York, allowed me to share in front of the congregation. Pastor Anderson's message can be heard by attending the church, or by listening to WLIX radio. On both of these occasions, what I had to share was heard by all who were present, as well as those listening to the live broadcast. I greatly appreciate having had those two opportunities to share. However, I do not want to ask him every time I'm in church. I'm not trying to monopolize anyone's time. You have, however, given me plenty to share. I have been praying for venues and opportunities to open up for a few years, to no avail. So why have you let so few venues open up for me to speak to others? I don't know the reason why...but nobody can silence my written word. So I decided to begin writing a book.

Chapter 1

I was born a normal healthy child, the youngest of three daughters. However, when I was two and a half years old, my mother noticed that physically there was something wrong with me. My parents brought me to numerous doctors. The common response from all the doctors we went to was that my Mom was just an "Over-worried mother."

The next few years of my life were very painful, and I know I have blocked out many memories from that period of time. But I will share what I do remember.

I began having spasms and involuntary movements throughout my body. Walking became difficult. One foot and the opposite arm were turning in, and not working correctly. Then the other foot and arm started to do the same thing. I began walking bowlegged. I developed lockjaw, and my body became so contorted that I looked like a pretzel. The progression rapidly continued. Because I could no longer sit or walk, I began lying on the couch all day, every day. I was in a lot of pain.

I think it was at this point that I started sleeping in my parent's bed. Every night one of my parents would have to lie on top of me in order to keep me as still as possible. By doing this, it helped to keep my pain level at a minimum. In the meantime, my other parent would sleep on the folding bed, just to get a little rest.

Around the age of four, I was diagnosed with Dystonia. In a nutshell, Dystonia is a condition that negatively affects the Central Nervous System. The brain sends the wrong messages to the muscles. For about the next two years, I went to Columbia Presbyterian Babies Hospital, and the doctors tried many different experimental medications. Each time I was in the hospital, it was for six or seven weeks at a time. This was so the doctors could monitor my progress. The medications did not help, and my condition worsened. The doctors at Columbia told my parents that I would need surgery. My parents took me to see Dr. Irving Cooper at Saint Barnabas Hospital in Bronx, New York. At the time he was considered to be the best brain surgeon in the world for the type of surgery I required.

When I was six years old, Dr. Cooper told my parents that he could not operate on me because the patient needs to be awake during surgery. The reason for this was so that he could see if what he was doing was effective in helping the patient. Because of my young age, Dr. Cooper did not want to operate on me. He said I would be too scared to stay awake for the surgery. My parents pleaded with him to do the surgery, because they did not want their baby daughter to die.

Dr. Cooper had the anesthesiologist use an anesthesia that put me to sleep. But he was able to wake me up when he needed to check the effectiveness, and then put me right back to sleep again.

My father told me that he and my mother knew I was fine when the elevator doors opened and they heard me yelling, "I want my mommy."

When I was in my bed in the hospital room, I asked my mother to scratch my nose. She said, "Scratch it yourself." My left arm moved my left hand and fingers up to my nose and I scratched my nose by myself. We were thrilled and amazed!

Chapter 2

My entire left side worked better. We were overjoyed, because we had not experienced this for the last few years. Our overwhelming feelings of joy only lasted for three days. We don't know why, but the Dystonia returned full force on my left side. I returned to see Dr. Cooper and another surgery was planned for my left side. As far as I can remember, I took it like a trooper. I had no idea that brain surgeries could be extremely dangerous. As far as I was concerned, my first surgery had been a breeze and this one would be as well. I woke up in the recovery room with a pounding, splitting headache. As far as I know, pain medication had not been administered to me. I was left with no choice but to just cry, and cry, and cry.

The nurse who was supposed to take care of me was really mean. She kept telling me in a nasty voice to stop crying. When I continued to cry, she became annoyed, and she told me that by crying, I was just making the pain worse. That stopped me from crying, but to this day I'm not convinced she was telling me the truth. My left side was better. It was less spastic, with fewer involuntary movements, and better muscle control. Shortly after the second surgery, when I was around seven years old, it was time to go to work on my right side.

The surgery that Dr. Cooper performed on my right side worked, but not as well as we hoped. Before any of these surgeries my speech was fine. My speech was negatively affected, because in order to do these operations, Dr. Cooper had to go through the speech center in my brain. I thank God that my parents made the decision for me to have these surgeries. What good is having clear speech if I was going to be immobile and in pain my entire life, if I even lived.

Going back to my right side. My parents spoke to Dr. Cooper about a second surgery for my right side. They decided against it when Dr. Cooper told him that he would do another surgery, but it could have taken away all of my ability to speak. Right choice again Mom and Dad.

I would like to end this chapter with a nice story.

I was not in a pediatric unit. My head had to be totally shaved for each surgery. For one of these surgeries, I was still in the hospital on October 31st. My father held me and carried me from room to room, bald, and I said, "Trick or treat." Everyone thought I was so cute and they each gave me a candy. I had a lot of fun, and by the time I returned to my room, I had a lot of candy!

Chapter 3

When I was about eight years old, my parents, my mother's sister, Aunt Millie and her husband, Uncle Zeke and I went to the beach on a warm, sunny afternoon. At the beach, my father carried me into the water in his arms. We stayed in the water for a while, and when we decided to go back to the family, my father was just about to walk out of the water, and somehow the water knocked him down. I fell, and my face was under the water just enough that I could have drowned. My neck muscles were not strong enough for me to lift my head above the water, but I could feel my father's right hand holding onto my right ankle. I had full confidence in my father. He was not going to let anything bad happen to me, so I patiently and calmly held my breath while I waited for him to pick me up. What I did not know at the time was that every time my father tried to get up, the water knocked him down again. My Uncle Zeke saw all of this, and God used Uncle Zeke to rescue me. Just as I was a split second away from suffocating or drowning, Uncle Zeke lifted me up out of the water. I thank God for watching over me that day, as He does everyday.

Chapter 4

After I had my third brain surgery, there was yet another problem. My right hand was closed into a fist, and I was unable to open it. On top of that, my right arm was moving in such a way that my right hand kept hitting the outside of my stomach. This did not hurt my stomach, but from what my parents have told me, all that hitting against my skin caused an indentation. This indentation kept getting bigger, and would have eventually worn away all the skin in that one spot. This would have left the inner part of my stomach exposed if allowed to continue.

Another visit to Dr. Cooper to see how he could help. I only remember lying in the hospital bed the night before the surgery. I also remember my parents going out into the hall to speak with the doctors who were there that evening. I knew that I was going to have surgery, but nobody filled me in on the details. At the time, the best hope that Dr. Cooper could offer my parents to alleviate this problem was another surgery. Unfortunately, that would have permanently paralyzed my entire right side. Years later, when I was old enough to understand, my parents explained to me that they questioned, "How can we do this to our daughter?" The doctors replied, "You have to listen to the doctor." My parents decided, against the doctor's advice, to not go through with the surgery. They checked me out of the hospital that evening, and the surgery was never rescheduled. I remember lying down in the back seat with my father holding me and looking perplexed. He was probably wondering if he and my mother had made the right decision.

Since my parents made the decision to not go forward with the surgery, they were still faced with the challenge of what to do next. Would they eventually have to take me back to Dr. Cooper to have the surgery anyway? Since the surgery was really the only option, they just didn't know what to do.

I did not find out until my late twenties or early thirties that my father continued to pray for a solution to this situation. Two weeks later, my arm and hand stopped hitting and wearing away my skin. Thank God for answered prayer!

Chapter 5

After all of that, I still had a clenched right hand that would not open for anything. The doctors still did not know how to help me. Then, unbeknownst to me at the time, my father read an article in the New York Times about someone who had a condition (not Dystonia), that was also extremely difficult to treat. The doctors did not know how to help this person either. Eventually, this person found a doctor who knew acupuncture. Finally, through acupuncture, God mightily helped this person.

My father contacted this doctor and explained my symptoms and situation. The doctor told my father "No," because he did not know if he could help me. "Please try," my father requested. Again the doctor said no, because the situation sounded too complicated. My father pleaded with him, "Please, just try to help my baby daughter." The doctor again refused, but he did give my father the name of another M.D. who administered acupuncture, Dr. Alfred Peng. After my father spoke to Dr. Peng, and he agreed to meet with us, my mother asked me if I would like to try acupuncture. I never heard of acupuncture before, so I asked her what it was. She told me the doctor would place needles in my skin, but that they would not hurt or make me bleed. I agreed to try it.

The first time I went to see Dr. Peng he administered acupuncture to me. During the treatment he saw the slightest bit of movement in my right fingers. My parents and I did not see any movement at all. A month later, I returned for my second visit. WHILE THE NEEDLES WERE STILL IN ME, all of my fingers opened up, and to this day I can still open my right hand. Praise God!!!

Although I continued to go once a month for about eight more months, there was no further progress during that period of time. Despite what I was told, some of the needles did hurt. There didn't seem to be any point in continuing treatment anymore. Since that time, I have tried acupuncture at several different seasons in my life, but it never helped relieve any more symptoms of Dystonia.

CHAPTER 6

Let's fast-forward nine years to June 9, 1981 when I was seventeen years old. Before I discuss June 9, 1981, I need to provide some background information.

The Dystonia had been extremely cruel to me, including in my jaw. The Dystonia had caused my facial muscles to pull my jaw way out of alignment. Because of that, the top of my jaw extended way out forward, the bottom jaw just hung down, and only the back two teeth on each side met. I could not chew the way most people do. The way I chewed was by taking the food and slapping it against the roof of my mouth with my tongue, until the food was soft enough to swallow. I'm sure it was not pleasant to watch me eat because I could not close my lips while I was eating. In addition to that, I had a constant, continual drool, because I was not able to close my lips. This was the case, whether I was eating or not.

For the most part, no one other than my family, teachers, and close friends could understand my speech. And often times, even they could not understand without great effort on both our parts. This was the impetus in my decision to correct this problem.

My mother brought me to an orthodontist at Long Island Jewish Hospital, and after his evaluation, he told us I would need jaw reconstruction surgery. I was referred to Dr. Stephen Sachs, an oral maxillofacial surgeon. Dr. Sachs told me I would need braces before the surgery, so he sent us to Dr. Richard Faber, an orthodontist. Dr. Faber applied braces in 1980, and I had the braces for a year before Dr. Sachs operated on my jaw. They operated through the inside of my mouth and I never had any scars on the outside.

The surgery required that every bone in my jaw be broken and reset. The surgery lasted almost eight hours. When I awoke from the anesthesia, I was in a lot of pain. It was not fun, and we'll leave it at that.

A few days later I looked at myself in the mirror and cried as I saw a smaller, prettier face. I would like to thank all of the speech/language pathologists who worked with me both before and after the surgery. Some of them worked with me for many years after my surgery. They deserve a lot of credit for their efforts, guidance, and support.

A History Maker

By ABBY AVIN BELSON
New York Times (1923-Current file); Sep 5, 1982;
ProQuest Historical Newspapers The New York Times (1851 - 2006)
pg. LI 12

Facial Surgery Brings New Hope

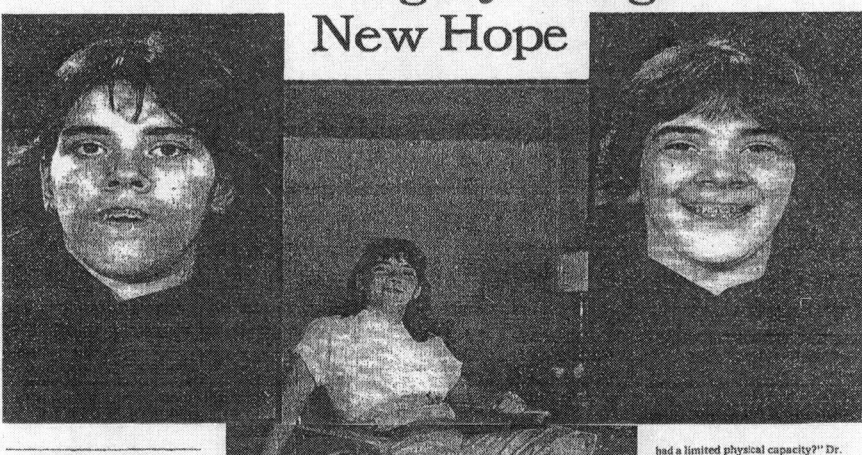

By ABBY AVIN BELSON

DIX HILLS

"I DON'T have a great deal of control over my destiny, but this was one choice I did have," said 18-year-old Laurie Ornstein of Dix Hills. The choice she was talking about was orthognathic surgery, a dramatic new operation that corrects facial deformities by cutting and repositioning bone.

Since the age of 4, Miss Ornstein has suffered from dystonia, a rare neurological disorder that produces excessive muscle activity in the arms, legs, torso and head. Continued activity, which is thought to be caused by faulty brain signals, may, in time, permanently distort the affected areas.

Miss Ornstein's illness has left her unable to use her legs and only partly able to use her arms. It is also believed to be responsible for an abnormally developed jaw that prevented her from closing her mouth.

The resulting problems were embarrassing. Studies have shown that many dystonia victims have above-average intelligence. "But when your mouth is always open, you drool uncontrollably, and people think you're retarded," said Miss Ornstein, who last year was elected to the National Honor Society for high school students.

"Eating is also hard," she said, "because food keeps falling out of your mouth. At school, there was a kid who always left the lunch table when I sat down. When I asked a friend why, she said, 'He can't stand watching you eat.'"

Perhaps the worst problem was the way she spoke. Although her speech defect is partly the result of difficulties in motor coordination, being unable to close her mouth made it impossible to pronounce p's, b's and m's. "People would talk to my mother instead of me," she said. "And if I answered the phone, anyone who didn't know me would hang up."

Laurie Ornstein, top, before and after orthognathic surgery, and relaxing at home in Dix Hills

The speech problem brought Miss Ornstein to the department of dentistry at the Long Island Jewish-Hillside Medical Center. "I thought braces might help," she said. At the hospital she was told about orthognathic surgery. According to Dr. Stephen Sachs, chief of oral and maxillofacial surgery, Long Island Jewish-Hillside is one of about 50 centers in the country with an extensive orthognathic program.

"Orthognathic surgery is different from plastic surgery, which deals with soft tissue," Dr. Sachs said. "There are cosmetic benefits from our operations. But they are done mainly to improve oral function in people with defects. The treatment of these defects involves teamwork between a surgeon and an orthodontist who together plan the necessary changes in bone and teeth."

"Recent advances in orthognathic treatment have made dramatic improvements possible," Dr. Sachs added. "While doctors have long known how to operate on the lower jaw, about 10 years ago they developed procedures for the upper jaw too. Now they can lengthen or shorten a face or move parts of it in any direction. All work is done through the mouth so there are no scars."

"When I first heard about the operation, I was shocked," said Miss Ornstein, who has had brain surgery for dystonia three times. "I didn't want any more pain, but I decided to go ahead because there was no other way to improve."

Although her parents supported her decision, the surgeon was more hesitant. "My first reaction was, what would we gain by operating on someone who couldn't communicate and had a limited physical capacity?" Dr. Sachs said. "I also had medical questions. In the past, most dystonia victims died in childhood. Now, thanks to new treatments, many reach adulthood. By then, the disease is usually no longer life-threatening. But since adult dystonia victims and orthognathic treatment are both so new, far as we could tell no one with dystonia had ever had the operation before."

Authorities whom Dr. Sachs consulted agreed that Miss Ornstein did not face abnormally dangerous health risks during or immediately after the operation. But there was the chance that continued muscle activity later on might distort the jaw once again.

"When we explained the risks to Laurie, it was clear that she wanted us to stop talking," Dr. Sachs said. "Her determination helped us decide to go ahead."

He remembers exactly when the decision was made. "There was a staff conference during which everyone discussed the pros and cons of operating. But when Laurie entered the room in her motorized wheelchair, something about her manner ended all objections."

The surgery planned for Miss Ornstein involved shortening her face by removing a segment from the upper jaw and raising it. Then the lower jaw would be moved back so the mouth could close properly. Like everyone who undergoes orthognathic surgery, she would need braces for several months before the operation to make certain her teeth were correctly positioned.

Once orthodonture was completed, the six-hour operation was scheduled for June 9, 1981. This date would allow Miss Ornstein to be well enough to attend her graduation several weeks later from the Human Resources School in Albertson.

Even more important to her was that wires that must hold the upper and lower jaw together for 10 weeks after surgery would be removed in time for her to enter Hofstra University.

15

Chapter 7

In September 1992, when I was twenty-eight years old, I had a gynecological appointment. This appointment with Dr. Z was a few days after I started my period. The doctor said she felt a lump in my right breast. Ordinarily she would think it was nothing, but because she felt it so soon after I started my period, she wanted me to have it checked.

Dr. Z asked if I had a surgeon. I did, we'll call him Dr. M. I had been going to him annually since I was sixteen for regular breast exams. I went to Dr. M, and he asked me why I was there. I told him that Dr. Z felt a lump, but I purposely did not tell him which side. Not only did he find it was the right side, but he found the exact lump in the exact same place that Dr. Z found it. According to Dr. M, he thought I was too young to have breast cancer, so he decided to "watch" it.

Meanwhile, my sister Karen, who is ten years older than me, also had a lump at the same time, and also went to Dr. M. Karen's lump was removed by him, and was found to be cancerous. She decided to have a lumpectomy at North Shore University Hospital in Manhasset, New York. That surgery was followed by radiation therapy, also at NSUH.

Dr. M had me come back to his office three or four times during the next eleven months, from September 1992. In August of 1993 he told me that the lump needed to be removed. I knew he was going to say that, but I was still shocked and distraught. I began crying and arguing with him. "I thought you told me it's not cancer," I said. "It's not," he replied. So then I asked him, "Why are you taking it out?" He said, "We can't be sure unless we do a biopsy." "But I thought you said it's not cancer," I insisted. Dr. M remained calm, but this circular arguing went on for a good solid twenty minutes.

The surgery for the biopsy was scheduled for Tuesday, September 7th, 1993. Before the surgery, Dr. M told me again not to worry, that it was not cancer. This entire set of circumstances was frustrating and confusing for me. I couldn't understand how in one breath he could tell me it's not cancer, and then follow that with telling me he could not be sure without the biopsy. When I awoke in my room, I felt so good, had no pain, and now the biopsy was finally done. I was being positive, and told myself I did not have cancer. I wanted to go to the mall to shop. The nurse had to interfere and tell my parents that going to the mall was not a good idea. A lot of people feel fine and go out and they are not fine. She told my parents to take me home, and that I should not go out for the rest of the day. Bummer! I went home, and I felt completely fine the entire day. I was doing so well that when my sister Karen arrived home at nine p.m. and looked at me she said, "You don't look like you had surgery today." I replied, "I don't feel like I did!"

The next day, September 8th, my mother and I went shopping at the mall. We sat down to have lunch, and while we were eating,

A History Maker

she told me that she was going to call the house. I asked her why. She told me she just wanted to make sure everything was all right. I reassured her that everything was all right. My mother went to a pay phone in the restaurant, I'm not sure if cell phones had even been invented yet. The pay phone was in a location where I could neither see nor hear her. She came back smiling and told me everything was fine. But I already knew that.

When we arrived home, my mother sat down on the couch and told me, "You have cancer." In shock and disbelief I asked, "What?" as I started to cry. She said, "Dr. M's office called the house while we were out and told Daddy that you have cancer." I couldn't believe it! Mom continued, "After I hung up with Daddy, I called Dr. M. He told me you have cancer."

"But he told you, Daddy, and me that I did not have cancer."

"He was wrong."

Shocked, stunned, and confused…I went into my room and cried for I don't know how long. Intuitively, somehow I knew that it had been caught early, so I was not afraid that my life was in jeopardy. I cried some more. "Why God? Why me? Haven't I been through enough in my short twenty-eight years? Now I have to deal with breast cancer also?" I continued crying.

That night, after I had already been calm for a few hours, my father asked if there was anything he could do for me. I could have asked for the world and he would have given it to me; that's how much he longed to ease my pain. I had one simple request. I asked him to call the Rabbi and let him know. And he did.

Even though I did not yet know Jesus, I still had spiritual acuity. I knew that if God was not included in my healing, then going to the best doctors and receiving the best treatments at the best hospitals would mean nothing!

The next twenty days were crazy. I had to gather as much information as I possibly could in a short amount of time and quickly decide my next step in the process. Let's just say that so much happened; I was so busy, my schedule so hectic and crazy, plus I had a lot of emotional pain, that I would not doubt if I blocked out from my mind certain things that happened.

On September 15th, 1993, I went to see a breast surgeon from Long Island Jewish Hospital. I'll call her Dr. Y. I liked her, and she said she would perform a lumpectomy, and take out some lymph nodes to see how much the cancer had spread. She answered all of my questions to my satisfaction, and I was happy with her. We scheduled the surgery for Tuesday, September 28th, 1993.

I still decided to go for another opinion. For the most part, my mother was trying to convince me to let Dr. M, the original surgeon, perform the operation. She felt that he was a good surgeon. I told her that he's not a breast surgeon, and that both she and my father had always taught me that when something is seriously wrong, you go to the top doctor at a top teaching hospital. On Friday, September 17th, 1993, I went to see Dr. Press (not his real name) who, at that time, was associated with one of the finest hospitals in Manhattan.

The first neurologist I ever had, as well as my supervisor at work, (they did not know each other) both recommended Dr. Press. Of all the breast surgeons in the New York Metropolitan area, two people who do not know each other both recommended Dr. Press. I figured he must be great!!!! Wrong!!!!

The exam Dr. Press gave me included an evaluation of how high I could lift my right arm. At that time, I could not lift my right arm high at all. After the exam, my mother met me in his office for his opinion. I was certain he would say the same thing as Dr. Y from Long Island Jewish Hospital. Authoritatively, both in posture and tone of voice (and maybe even a touch of arrogance) he said matter-of-factly, "You have no choice but to have a mastectomy." I wanted to burst out crying, but I held it in until I was out of his sight. No apologies, and certainly no bedside manners. My mother asked him, "What about a lumpectomy?" He replied, "Can't do a lumpectomy because she can't lift her arm high enough to receive radiation treatments after the surgery." The rest of the conversation was a total blur. To say I was devastated is putting it mildly.

We left religious services early on the second day of Rosh Hashana. For what? For this idiot? I was crying. He had spoken so authoritatively that I thought perhaps he was correct. I cried and cried, and cried some more.

We decided to speak to the first surgeon, Dr. Y, to hear what she had to say. My mother would not have her paged because, according to her, it was not an emergency. I thought it was, but since I was in such a bad frame of mind, I did not have the oomph or wherewithal to argue with her. So that weekend was probably the worst weekend of my life. I cried, and when I was not crying outwardly, I was crying inwardly.

Monday morning my mother left a message for Dr. Y to call us back. I was sitting on pins and needles the whole day waiting for the call. That evening, I went to my Jewish Singles Social Group at the YM-YWHA. She still hadn't called back, and I figured that going out might help take my mind off the situation. It helped a little. After about two and a half hours, my father came to take me home. "Did the doctor call?" was the first thing out of my mouth as soon as I saw him.

"Yes."

"What did she say?"

"I don't know, you'll have to ask your mother."

That drive seemed to take forever. As soon as I went in the house, I saw my mother.

"What did the doctor say?"

"She said you don't need a mastectomy…"

Waves of relief came over me. Silently I thanked God. My mother continued…

"The doctor asked me if we had gone to see another doctor. I told her yes."

"What happened?" the doctor asked my mother. "I'll tell you another time."

No one ever told me this, but I know my mother, and when the doctor told her "No," I can see that she broke down crying hysterically. The doctor probably wanted to help her with whatever she had been experiencing. When my mother said, " I'll tell you another time," she was probably crying so hysterically that she couldn't talk about it at that moment in time.

That was September 20th and the surgery was scheduled for September 28th. I did the best I could to keep active and busy, but nothing totally distracted me from my upcoming lumpectomy. In fact, the closer the surgery came, the less and less I was able to be distracted. I knew that once I had the lumpectomy I would be fine. It was the waiting that was torturous.

September 28th, 1993, the day had finally arrived! My mother had pre-purchased the movie "Alladin" for me. September 28th, 1993, was the day that Disney had decided to release the video for arrival in stores for pick-up. Since I did not have to be at the hospital until late morning or early afternoon, my mother drove me to the mall so I could pick up my movie before I had the surgery. I have a feeling that she wanted me to be happy and have a good feeling before I had surgery.

We left the mall and went straight to the hospital. When my mother and I arrived, I went into the lobby and my sister Aileen was there with my nephew Gabriel, who was a year and a half old at the time. Gabriel was holding a small Mylar balloon that had a pretty design and the words "Get Well Soon." He ran over eagerly and gave me the balloon. I started thinking that he was the reason I had to get better. I loved him so much! If he was this sweet at a year and a half, I had to see him grow up to be a fine man.

I went upstairs and changed into one of those flimsy hospital gowns. Doctors were talking to me, asking me all kinds of medical history questions. A few days prior, I had been at LIJ, and requested that their Rabbi come visit me. While I was speaking with these doctors, the Rabbi came in. I was embarrassed because I thought I would see him while I was fully clothed. He asked me for my Hebrew name and for my mothers' Hebrew name. I told him and he said he would say a prayer for me. I thanked the Rabbi, and he left.

The doctors continued their conversation with me. When we were finished talking, they took me to the pre-op waiting area. The surgeon came in and spoke with my parents and me. Then she handed me a consent form to sign. With all of the surgeries I had in the past, this was the first time I was old enough to sign the consent form for myself. It was only then that I had, for the first time, an appreciation for the difficult times my parents had been through signing the consent form for surgery for me so many times before.

I just love it when doctors are so arrogant that they think they know a patients body better than the patient knows her own body.

The surgeon was in the O.R. along with two student doctors. She told one of them to start the IV. I was trying to be helpful and told him where I had a good vein. Did he go there? No. I told him the same thing again. Did he listen to me? No. He tried a totally different place and that did not work either. Now I was annoyed and started yelling, "Why won't you listen to me? I know where I have a good vein!" The surgeon intervened and told the other doctor to try. He put it in exactly where I said and it worked like a charm. I started yelling at the other doctor, "You see, if you had listened…" I was in dreamland.

That night was tough. I was in pain, and I was sick. By the time the surgery had begun, it was four p.m. The next morning when the surgeon came to see me at nine a.m. she told me that it was time for me to go home. I told her that I was still feeling queasy, and she said I could stay another night, but that I would have to go home the next day.

I did go home the next day, but I was in pain. The pain was not from the surgery, surprisingly, but from the drain. I had no choice but to deal with the pain, and the drain would come out in a few days.

On October 1st, 1993, a woman who worked in the surgeon's office called. My mother answered the phone. The woman told my mother that the surgeon's office had just received my report, and the report could not have been any better! Everything had worked out perfectly! I cried as I thanked God!!!

A few points of interest I did not mention during this chapter:

The results from the lumpectomy showed that Dr. M had removed all of the cancer during the biopsy. Even though Dr. M had left the lump for a year, it was still only at stage one when it was removed. What a mighty and wonderful God we serve! On December 23rd, 2009, I celebrated sixteen years of being cancer free!! Praise the Lord!!!!!!

Chapter 8

After the breast surgeon removed the drain, she told me to recover for a couple of weeks and then it would be time for me to receive radiation therapy. She gave me the name of a doctor I could have gone to in Plainview, very close to where I was living, or I could go to LIJ. Thankfully, she said I did not need chemotherapy.

A couple of weeks later my mother brought me to a male doctor in Plainview. Then from there we went to LIJ where we met with a female doctor. Even though she was much farther from my home, she was also much more personable and easy to talk to. Besides, I would only have to go for thirty treatments with her, and the male doctor told me I would have to come for thirty-three treatments. I wondered why there was a discrepancy, but I never asked. I kept my mouth shut and went for the thirty treatments.

Both of these doctors told me that the radiation would not hurt, but very soon after treatment began, I experienced pain in my breast and I thought something was very wrong! I ran to my doctor and told her. She told me not to worry, that it was normal. I wondered why she had told me it would not hurt when she knew full well it would.

During my treatments she asked me, "I know you only needed a lumpectomy but were you ever even offered the option of a mastectomy?" I told her the story of what happened with Dr. Press and she was fuming!

A couple of observations I have had in my mind ever since I went for radiation therapy. The first is that everyone who worked in that department was genuinely nice. Even my sister Karen, who had gone to a nearby hospital for her treatments made the same observation about everyone who worked where she had gone. That was nice. To be going through such a difficult time in one's life and to be surrounded with only nice, caring people. It was a pleasure.

The second observation:

Since I was not able to get myself on and off the table, two of the people who administered the radiation lifted me up to put me on the table, and then lifted me up again to sit me back in my wheelchair when the treatment was done. It was not always the same two people. In fact, they took turns. All of the people who administered the radiation, both male and female lifted me. When they would lift me up, I was higher than the pockets of their white coats, so I was able to see inside their pockets. It amazed and shocked me that about ninety-five percent of them carried a pack of cigarettes in their pockets!

Before I receive many letters, I will say that these people must have an extremely stressful job. To work with cancer patients eight hours a day, five days a week must be difficult. That's the reason I could not understand why so many of them smoked. Did they think that because they treated cancer patients that they would be exempt from getting cancer? I do not know what they were thinking, and I am not judging them, it was just an observation I made along with some accompanying thoughts.

Chapter 9

That's enough about the surgeries for a while. I have been looking forward to writing this chapter, my salvation testimony.

Looking back with twenty/twenty hindsight I realize that there were many people who tried to evangelize me, and I would never let them. I am sure many, if not all of them prayed for my salvation.

My story begins as a second semester freshman at Hofstra University. This was my first semester living in the dorm. Diane was my main aide for two and a half years. I knew she was a Christian, but that did not bother me because I had been taught to love everyone no matter what religion, ethnicity, color…the individual happened to be.

I had learned about Judaism from some of the best Rabbi's who ever lived. My knowledge of and love for Judaism at that point had been great, and my love of the Lord (not Jesus) had been even greater. I loved the Lord and I did my best to please the Lord about seventy-five percent of the time.

It did not take long for me to realize that all Diane would ever talk about was Jesus, Jesus, and more Jesus. I thought to myself, doesn't

Diane know haw to have a normal conversation about anything without including Jesus? Diane wouldn't even talk about how nice the weather was without mentioning Jesus.

I was convinced that Diane was downright wrong and brainwashed. I was going to show her just how ridiculous her thinking and beliefs were. She would come out with the most ridiculous statements. "Jesus was born to a virgin" and "Jesus rose from the dead" were two of them. Respectfully, I asked her, "How can a virgin become pregnant?" or "How could she believe that anyone rose from the dead?" Not only did she have an answer for these questions, but when I would ask her about things, it would always lead her to additional topics. Topics ranging from Jesus, His life, ministry, what He taught and why, His death and resurrection, as well as topics I haven't even mentioned. My beliefs in Judaism were still extremely strong, and I was still convinced that Diane was downright wrong!

Diane had Christian students as friends. I did not have many friends, as I was still a newcomer to Hofstra University, so Diane's friends became my friends. One of Diane's friends, J.P., a sweet young college student who was very much like Diane in that she too, only spoke about Jesus. I tried to show them the error of their ways, but they just did not understand.

Mary Ann and Amy were two more of Diane's friends. Somewhere along the line I became convinced that Diane was trying to convert me. When I would ask her about this, she would usually downplay or deny that she was trying to convert me. I was also convinced that J.P., Mary Ann, and Amy were all engaged in a conspiracy with Diane to convert me. I found it refreshing when one evening, Amy joined me in the cafeteria for dinner. It was just the two of us. Amy told me that she wanted me to become a Christian so that I could know the joy that she experienced from knowing Jesus. Finally, someone admitted she was trying to convert me. I breathed a sigh of relief.

I still knew they were all crazy!!! I should have realized something was up when Diane invited me to go with her and J.P. to an Amy Grant concert. I accepted their invitation, figuring that although it was Christian Music, I could still enjoy it. Little did I know I would have to sit on my hands to prevent myself from raising them up in the air. After a while, even that didn't work, and I found myself raising my hands. I thought to myself, "What in the world are you doing?" I answered myself, "It's harmless!"

The whole Christian thing, no matter how much I learned about Christianity, still did not make any sense to me. Again, I should have known that Jesus was drawing me to Himself when Diane was going to church one Wednesday evening, and I felt the need to go with her. I asked Diane if she would take me with her, and without hesitation, she said, "Yes!"

I went to church that night and it was interesting, but I still thought they were crazy. I sought counsel from non-Christians whom I deeply admired and highly respected. They all basically told me to respect what the Christians believe, but most of these people agreed with me that most Christians had a few marbles missing. However, I was still standing strong in my Judaism. I could not believe that no matter what question I posed and no matter how I tried to prove them wrong, they always had an answer and I could never seem to shake them.

All of this went on for about a year and a half before I started thinking about what they believed and wondering if they were actually correct. "Shake yourself out of it," I would say suddenly to myself many times over the course of the next year.

I started asking more questions about Jesus and Christianity. It still did not make sense, but nonetheless, I felt my solid foundation of Judaism sinking right out from under my feet. I became confused.

After two and a half years of having been preached to, I finally decided enough was enough. I hired a different aide, and I did not have any more contact with the Christian friends I had made. I was Jewish, and I was going to remain Jewish. I needed time to clear my head from all the junk. As far as I was concerned, if I never had any contact with another Born-Again Christian for as long as I lived it would be too soon!!

★★

I spent the next few years being confused. Had I been wrong all my life? Were the Christians truly correct? Is Jesus the Messiah…?

I did not know who to turn to, so finally around the age of twenty-five I prayed, "Lord, do You want me to believe in Jesus? I do not know what to do. Whatever You want, I will do." I sought the Lord for a long time on this question. He told me He wanted me to remain Jewish. I thought, felt, and believed that He meant that I was not to believe in Jesus.

I had my answer. Good. Now I could move forward with my life without all of those questions plaguing and haunting me. Then in 1994, I joined a dating service. I chose the profile of Mike (not his real name). Mike let the dating service know that he would like to meet me. The dating service gave us each other's phone numbers. We called each other and agreed to meet each other for lunch on Sunday, July 24th. (For people who meet this way, I strongly recommend meeting in a public place. Mike and I met at a restaurant).

On Mike's profile, he listed "Christian" as his religion. I thought nothing of that because I knew that so many people called themselves

Christian, and Jesus meant very little if anything at all to them. It did not disturb me that Mike identified himself as a Christian.

We dated the rest of July, and all of August and September. The first Sunday evening in October when we went out for dinner, I asked Mike, "What kind of Christian are you?" He looked at me with a blank stare and answered simply, "Christian." "I know, but are you Lutheran, Presbyterian…" Now he understood what I was asking. He replied, "Born Again."

Shocked, I looked up toward Heaven and I said a quick prayer. "Lord, this is not funny. You know I want to marry Mike. You also know I never wanted to see or be in contact with another Born Again Christian for the rest of my life!"

Why was I shocked? Mike never really spoke about Jesus, and when he did, he didn't beat me over the head with the Bible. He did not try to convert me. We used to have great discussions about comparative religion, and I always felt that Mike respected that not only was I Jewish, but that I was committed to my faith. I also found it refreshing that we could and did have these religious discussions without him trying to convert me.

Mike and I continued to date. As time went on, our conversations became more intense, still respectful, but much more intense. I finally realized that Mike's religion was so important to him that I did not stand a chance of becoming his wife if I were not a Christian.

I did not know what to do. I wanted to remain Jewish, but I loved Mike so much and I wanted to marry him.

I figured out what to do. I made up a convoluted salvation testimony with lots of twists and turns in it (the way most people's salvation testimonies are). I'll remain Jewish, and Mike will never know the difference.

This had to be good. And it had to be convincing. I spent at least a month thinking up a good convoluted salvation testimony. I am not recommending that anyone else do what I did. I went against God's commandment, "Thou shalt not lie." Honesty is always the best policy.

In January 1995, I told Mike I had salvation. He was curious to hear how I'd been saved, so I told him my story. He sat and questioned me for an hour. It wasn't that he did not believe me. Mike wanted to make certain I knew what I was doing.

I learned so much from the Christians almost fifteen years prior to this, that no matter what question Mike asked me, I knew exactly the right answer. After an hour Mike was convinced that I knew Jesus in a personal way as my Lord and Savior.

Mike had been attending a Bible study every other week, but he never invited me to go with him. Now that he believed I knew Jesus, Mike asked me if I wanted to go with him to the Bible study. I answered, "Yes."

The Bible study was held in a certain couples' home. Everyone sat around in a circle in this couples' living room. After the study, people were asked for their prayer requests. I became nervous. I did not know how to pray for people. I listened intently. People would lift up others' prayer needs and when they were done praying the individual would say, "In Jesus' Name, Amen." Three people in a row prayed this way. I suddenly gained new confidence. "This is easy," I thought. My first time at Bible study and I was the fourth one to pray. At the end of my prayer I said, "In Jesus' Name, Amen." That was easy enough and no one had any idea I did not believe in Jesus. It was going to be easy to fool Mike and all the other Christians. I went with Mike to Bible study every time for four times in a row. Each time I prayed for people and then at the end, "In Jesus' Name, Amen."

This was great! No one knew. Then God convicted my heart. The Lord said to me, "You can't keep praying in Jesus' Name if you don't believe in Jesus." I knew He was serious and that He meant business. Never before had the Lord dealt so sternly with me.

Now I did not know what to do. I figured I had two choices. Either tell Mike the truth and definitely lose him, or try living as a Christian and see if it was a lifestyle that I would feel comfortable living. The latter choice sounded a whole lot better, and on April 29th, 1995, I (really) asked Jesus to come into my heart and be my personal Lord and Savior.

In October 1995, Mike and I ended our relationship, and now fifteen years later, I have never stopped loving Jesus.

Chapter 10

When I became Born Again, I knew I could not tell my parents, or anyone else in my family for that matter. They would have had a fit, to put it mildly.

Mike and I spent our time together going to Bible studies or fellowshipping with other Christians. My parents allowed Mike to drive me in their van. Now that Mike was no longer in the picture, I had no way of seeing my friends for any fellowship. I certainly could not ask my parents to drive me to Bible study, or God forbid, to church. I knew to not even bring a New Testament into my parents' home. All Hell would have broken loose if anyone were to find a New Testament in my possession. My parents did have a Bible in their home, but not a Bible that included the New Testament.

I wanted desperately to learn about Jesus. At that time my mother and I went to the mall almost every day. She and I would walk together for a while, and then I would tell her that I wanted some time alone. When we would part ways, I would race to the bookstore and read the New Testament. This occurred every time we went to the mall. I did not understand what I was reading and I did not yet know that I could ask Jesus for clarification and understanding of what I had read. However, it gave me great comfort and satisfaction to know that I could and did read Gods' Word in the New Testament everyday.

Even though I could not ask anyone in my family for a ride to visit with my Christian brothers and sisters, and even though I could not bring a New Testament into my parent's home, no one could stop me from praying to my newfound Lord, Jesus. And boy did I pray. I did not know how to pray, but I did not care. I prayed anyway.

I do not recall most of what I prayed for during that time. I do know that I prayed for Jesus to work out a way that I could find my own apartment so that I could worship him in the way that I saw fit.

I remember going into my room one night and asking God why I had this disability. At this point in my walk with the Lord I was such a baby Christian that I did not even know that people had to believe in Jesus in order to see and enter into Heaven. (See John 3) I just knew I loved Jesus. When I asked him this question, it was out of sheer curiosity. No anger was involved. He answered me quickly, "Laurie, I'm going to use you with your disability to bring your family to know me and to love me." I did not understand what Jesus meant. I did understand how much I loved Jesus and the fact that He was going to use me to bring my family to Him made me rejoice. I started thanking Him and praising Him for the disability.

Chapter 11

On March 7th, 1996, I received the long awaited phone call. My apartment would be available for me on April 1st. Did I want it? Without hesitation I answered "Yes!"

A lot needed to be done in those short twenty-four days. I contacted Social Services because I needed an increase in my daily hours for personal care. I placed an ad in local newspapers to find good, competent people to work for me. I had to interview the people who called. I called the phone company to set up my phone and they gave me my phone number. I had to call LIPA to make certain I had electric service. About a week before April 1st, my mother and I went shopping for everything I would need in my new apartment. These were just a few of the many things I had to accomplish before April 1st, 1996.

April 1st finally arrived and I was so excited! I moved in that evening and my family made four or five trips back to their home in order to bring all of my stuff to my new apartment.

Look what God did for me! April 1st was a Monday, and the following Sunday, April 7th was Easter Sunday. He had arranged my move so that my first Sunday in church would be Easter Sunday!

Now I had to find a church. I had called the phone company two weeks prior to moving, and they told me my phone service would be working on April 1st. It wasn't. I did not have phone service until late Wednesday afternoon. That gave me two days to find a church, because I also wanted to go on Good Friday.

First thing Thursday morning I called a local church to ask for help with transportation. They said they did not have anyone who could give me a ride. Now I did not know what to do. My aide suggested another local church. When I called this other church, the woman who answered the phone connected me to a pastor. I told the pastor what I needed. He told me that they had a ministry for the disabled and he had someone who could possibly give me a ride. He was going to get in touch with him and have him call me that day. When we hung up the phone I yelled, "Thank you Jesus!" I waited for this call all morning, afternoon, and night. No call! I called the same pastor first thing Friday morning. Very calmly I explained that I did not receive the call I had been waiting for. He told me I needed to be patient, because I had only called the day before. My blood was boiling, but God helped me to remain relatively calm. I said to him, "Today is Good Friday, and Sunday is Easter. How patient do you expect me to be?"

An hour later I received a phone call from Dave. "You need a ride to church? I can give you a ride to church." I asked him, "Can we go tonight?" He replied, "No, not tonight." "Oh," I replied disappointed. Dave said, "Let me come over tonight. We'll meet and get to know one another a little bit." Still disappointed, I said "Okay."

That evening I learned a truth that would continue the rest of my life. As soon as Dave walked through the door, I felt as if I'd known him my entire life. That has happened with most Christians I have met over the past fifteen years. Dave and I spoke for two hours. It was as if we had continued a conversation from the day before.

Easter Sunday morning Dave gave me a ride to church. It was great! It was what my soul and spirit had been longing for. Finally, I was in church not for a wedding or a baptism, but for me to worship my Lord and Savior Jesus! I must admit it did seem somewhat weird to me to be there for that reason. But it was great! The pastor's message was about Jesus' resurrection power. That was the beginning of almost nine years at that church.

Chapter 12

At that time, the church I attended gave a Bible to all first time visitors. I had to use my manual wheelchair because there was no way Dave could have maneuvered my motorized chair into his car. Dave wheeled me over to the Welcome Desk and introduced me to the person who was working behind the desk that day. That person handed me a NIV (New International Version) Bible. For the next three weeks, all I did all day long was read my Bible. And it was exactly that. My Bible. I now had my own apartment and did not have to answer to anyone but God, and if I felt like reading the New Testament, that's what I read. And I did not have to go to the bookstore anymore.

I was reading the New Testament for the first time (excluding the bookstore) and not understanding most of what I read. I read straight through the beginning of Matthew through the end of Revelation. I did not care, I just kept reading.

In the parts that I did comprehend, I was surprised to see how Jewish Christianity really is. Most churches, I have found, do not teach the Jewishness of Christianity. Now, fifteen years later, I have come to realize that most of the churches and ministries that do teach this, don't teach it correctly. Don't get me started. Let's leave it at most believers, both Jewish and Gentile, have very little if any knowledge of the Jewishness of Jesus and Christianity.

Growing up in a good Jewish home, I had been taught that Jesus had been Jewish, a Rabbi, and that most of the early church had been Jewish. That's where the discussion left off. I was always taught to believe that only Gentiles (non Jews), were Christians. I've since learned that's not the case. People from any religion, even agnostics and atheists, can become a Christian.

Anyway, I digressed. When I realized I had become a Born Again Christian, I wondered how and when I was going to tell my family. I did not know, and could not figure it out. I kept thinking, thinking…for months. Hmmmmm. Well, I thought, my parents really badly wanted to see me get married, even if the man I chose to marry would be a non-Jew.

I figured if I did not tell them I believed in Jesus until I was to be married, that it would cancel out all the pain they would feel. They would be so ecstatic about my upcoming marriage , and ultimately, they just want me to be happy. That was it! That was how I would handle this situation. Not tell them until I was ready to become married. Good idea!

But God had other plans. After I moved into my apartment, my brothers and sisters in Christ kept telling me to tell my parents. I couldn't. After much prodding, they practically urged me to tell my parents. I wasn't ready to tell them yet, so I didn't.

Between April 1st and July 2nd 1996, a series of events happened. Even if I tried, I wouldn't remember them all. They were little things like people leaving tracts (Religious pamphlets) in my front door, or people saying one or two sentences they would not say unless the person believed in Jesus. They would say these things to me in front of my parents. My parents are very intelligent people. I have learned it's difficult to keep a secret from them.

On Tuesday morning, July 2nd, 1996, my father was driving me from my parents' house back to my apartment. Dad had it all worked out in his mind already. He had a case, and presented it in such a way that took all of my possible excuses away from me. "So Laurie, what's going on?" he asked. I had absolutely no way out except to tell him the truth. I took a breath, paused, and braced myself for what would follow. The most difficult sentence I would ever have to speak. "I believe that Jesus is the Son of God." Those nine words were torturous for me to have to say to him, and I'm sure torturous for him to hear.

Let's just say that my father and I had words, and leave it at that. Those words upset me so much that I cried uncontrollably. I was hurt for myself and also for my father. Would he tell my mother? She would have a less than favorable response also.

That Saturday night, July 6th, 1996, my mother and I went out for the evening. When we returned home at midnight, she told me she needed to talk to me.

"Now?"

"Yes now!"

"But I'm tired and I need to go to sleep."

"We need to talk first."

My mother tried to convince me that I was wrong for believing in Jesus and she tried to talk me out of this "fad."

God must have been speaking through me because I did not yet know that much about Jesus and Christianity. But somehow, I had a response for every question she asked me. I kept looking at the clock because I had to wake up at 8 a.m. in order to be at church on time. I could see she was prepared to go all night if that's what she needed to do to convince me I was wrong. Finally, at 3:45 a.m. I told her, "I'm tired. I need to go to sleep."

The relationship between my parents and me became strained for about a year. They never stopped loving me, and they continued to help me in whatever way I needed. I never stopped loving them, and I kept praying and hoping our relationship would return to normal, even though they now knew the truth about me loving Jesus. I was not telling them that they had to believe in Jesus, I just wanted them to come to terms with what I had decided to believe.

Chapter 13

The next twelve months or so were extremely difficult. My parents would ask me questions that I did not know the answers to, and then when I would find out the answer, they did not want to hear it anymore. We cried a lot both over the phone and when we were together. Didn't I understand the pain they were going through? I tried very hard to reassure them that I did understand, but please don't ask me to give up believing in Jesus.

One day, about two months after they found out, my mother was over at my apartment. She found the book "Betrayed" written by Stan Telchin, hidden in my drawer. She asked me if she could borrow it. I answered, "Yes." She told me she wanted to see the kind of stuff I was reading.

A few weeks later, my parents came over. They had both read the book. My father called it "propaganda." I told him it's not propaganda, that it's his true story. They were hurt, and I was becoming really upset. I'll never forget how my mother, who was upset with my decision, took me and hugged me in her bosom when she saw how upset I was becoming. She also told my father to stop hounding me and to leave me alone. He left me alone then, but these heated discussions continued for a long while.

In February or March 1997, my father asked me to call a Rabbi and talk to him. This Rabbi specialized in helping peoples' children become deprogrammed from cults, and my parents had spoken to him about me. My father also explained to me that I would have to keep an open mind. "Can you do this for your mother and me?" I agreed.

A few days later, I called this Rabbi. He told me he was busy and asked if I could call him back. I asked him when, and he said to call him in about an hour. However, I did not call him back. I was the one who called him. I was the one who was asked to keep my mind open. I felt the least he could have done was take my number and call me back.

★★

How did I make it through this difficult time? The Lord Jesus, lots of prayer, and the love and support from my church family. I also had a strong support system from my brothers and sisters at Samantha's Li'l Bit of Heaven.

I can hear you wondering, "What is Samantha's Li'l Bit of Heaven?" It's a coffee house type of ministry for Christians (although everyone is welcome to come through the doors at "Heaven") where people love and encourage each other. We also pray for one another. People from all denominations, religions, and even agnostics and atheists are welcome.

Between my church family and my family at Heaven, all of my questions were patiently answered. They prayed for me, gave me a shoulder on which to cry, loved, encouraged, and supported me the whole way through this difficult journey.

My parents came to my apartment about a year after my father confronted me. This time they told me that although they were not happy with what I had come to believe, they just wanted me to be happy. Since they could see that I was happy, that's all that mattered to them.

In my heart I whispered to Jesus, "Praise God."

Chapter 14

Going back to May of 1996, I became bored. I did not want to sit home every night. It was a Thursday. I called Dave to see if he had any suggestions, and he told me about Samantha's Little Bit of Heaven. "Oh yeah?" I replied. He told me, "I can give you a ride there, but I can't give you a ride home. If you can find a ride home, I'll take you." I said, "I'll find a ride home." I was determined to find a ride home. I had to get out of the house and start fellowshipping with some people.

That evening, Dave gave me, and my manual wheelchair a ride to "Heaven." I will never forget that evening. There were only six or seven people there. Everyone seemed pleasant. Then somehow we all gathered around a table. There were a few of us sitting on one side, and a few other people sitting on the other side.

We were all talking and having a good time. Remember, this was my first time there, so no one knew me. Then there was a quiet hush in the room. This nice man Merrill, was sitting across from me. I was in my manual chair, leaning forward with my elbows on the table and my chin in my hands. The wheels of my manual wheelchair did not lock very well. Merrill started telling this long joke, and right before the punch line Merrill kept repeating the same line over and over again in order to buy himself time to remember the punch line. For some reason I found this hysterical and I began laughing so hard that my chair slipped out from under me and I fell on my back onto the floor. I was laughing so hard that no sound was coming out of me, and when I fell to the floor, my laughing stayed the same. I was not hurt, but no one there knew that at the time. They did not know if they should call 911 or what. "Laurie, are you all right?" someone asked. I was laughing so hard that I could not answer. "Laurie, I need to know if you're all right!" I couldn't answer. It was not until a few minutes later, when I needed to gasp for air, that some sound came out and they all realized I had been laughing the whole time. Samantha and I , and Merrill when he's around, still laugh about that night.

I have remained a regular at "Heaven" coming up on fourteen years. People from the New York Metropolitan area, people from all over the country and all across the globe have come to "Heaven." Some people come one time, some for a season, and there are a few of us who have remained regulars for many years. I have met many wonderful people at "Heaven" and I am grateful to the Lord Jesus for having provided "Heaven" on earth.

Chapter 15

One of the wonderful people I met at "Heaven" was Paul (not his real name). Paul is a very nice, sweet, Christian man. Back when I met Paul (I think it was 1997), he was timid and shy, and didn't say much of anything to anyone. He kept to himself.

Then as time went by, week after week, Paul would talk to me. Each week he would share a little more with me. We started having real conversations. I enjoyed Paul's company, and he enjoyed mine.

He also was a real gentleman. When "Heaven" was packed, Paul would give up his seat for a woman to sit down. I would have rather been sitting next to Paul, but it was nice to see that he was such a gentleman. He did a lot of little things like this, and when taken together, made a huge lasting impression on me.

Something else I noticed about Paul. He only talked and sat with me for about nine months. We had a wonderful relationship and I was head over heels in love with him. If Paul had asked me to marry him, I would have done so the following day. Then I noticed that Paul started sitting with other people. The other people were always only men. I thought, Wow, Paul really likes me, because he never sat with other women.

In April 1998, my friend Roseann married her husband Rick. I was invited to the wedding, and Paul went with me as my guest. In May 1998, my friend Tom married his wife Martina, and Paul came with me to their wedding also. When we arrived at the reception hall, we found out that the reception was upstairs. There was a flight of stairs, a landing, and then an even bigger flight if stairs. We asked where the elevator was…no elevator. I was shocked. Absolutely shocked.

The Americans with Disabilities Act (ADA) had been a law for at least seven years. Part of the ADA provides access to public places for everyone who has a disability, unless the business (i.e. mom and pop shop) or some other small business can show that making such accommodations would pose an "undue hardship." This was not the case with the catering hall/country club.

The men who worked there wanted to carry me up the stairs, while I was sitting in my power chair. I told them no. They insisted. I told them, "No, this chair is at least four hundred pounds, and even if I were to get out of the chair, the chair alone would still be too heavy." They said, "We do this all the time." My reply was, "No." I would not, and did not let them. Finally, they left me alone.

Paul and I were on the first floor looking at each other. Paul said, "What now?" I remembered something that my pastor taught in one of his sermons about a month or two earlier. "You can do more than pray after you have prayed, but you can do nothing until you have prayed." I grabbed Paul's hand and said, "Let's pray." We each prayed, and then Paul said, "I have an idea."

We were five minutes away by car from two local hospitals. Paul suggested he call one of the hospitals, tell someone there the situation, and ask if we could borrow a manual wheelchair. What a great idea! As he made the phone call I was praying that this would be the solution and that whoever he spoke to would be willing to help. Jesus answered our prayer with a "Yes" and an "Amen."

Paul told me he would be back in a few minutes. He returned with a manual wheelchair. I never dreamed that a manual wheelchair could look so beautiful! The men who worked there first carried the manual wheelchair up the stairs, and then me. When we got to the top of the stairs, they sat me in the wheelchair.

Then Paul and I went into the reception. Our table assignment was with two couples, friends of mine from the Bible study that I had attended with Mike. Paul and I had a nice time with these friends. A couple of hours later, both of these couples left, even though the reception was not yet over. That gave Paul and me the opportunity to have a somewhat private conversation. All of the other guests were busy talking amongst themselves.

We were having a very nice, innocent, sweet conversation. I was really enjoying myself. Finally Paul and I were really talking and getting to know each other. Then a nasty woman came over. I say that because she knew me, and she knew that I was the friend of Tom and Martina's, and that I brought Paul as my guest. I did not know at the time that she and Paul knew each other. She started talking to both of us, but mostly to Paul. Then she asked Paul, "Have you gone out with Yvette (not her real name) yet?" I was taken aback, and Paul was squirming. He knew he was my date for that night and he probably didn't want me to know about Yvette. He answered, "Yes, we went to the movies last night." My heart sank. She then said, "Good! Yvette is really nice." Paul replied, "Yes, she is." The woman continued, "I think she's a good woman for you." Talk about adding insult to injury, and then pouring salt on the open wound. Finally she left. I couldn't believe what I had just heard. I wanted to continue the nice conversation we had been having when we were so rudely interrupted! I did not talk about Yvette at all, and neither did Paul. I tried to suppress my feelings for the time we had left at the reception. We did have a nice conversation, but inside I was crying and dying.

When Paul drove me home, he told me how impressed he was with me because I had suggested that we pray when we didn't know how we were going to get upstairs. Had it been too little, too late?

CHAPTER 16

P aul and Yvette started dating and became boyfriend and girlfriend. Looking back, I know that something had not been right. Paul sat only with other men and me for a year. Although he liked me, I guess he did not like me enough to ask me out on a date. That should have been a huge indication to me to take a hint.

A few months before the whole incident happened at the wedding, I became depressed because Paul had not yet asked me to go out with him. I wanted to go for counseling. It so happened that I called a counselor who somehow knew Paul very well. When I explained some of what I was feeling, he told me, "Laurie, I'm not telling you this to hurt you." Oh great, now insult to injury to come again. He went on to say, "Paul thinks very highly of you, but he's not interested in you in that way. I'm telling you this so that you do not keep hoping that you might get him, and then when you don't, you'll be even more depressed."

The knife kept going in deeper and was becoming sharper. The depression was horrible! I could not sleep all night, every night. I would lie in bed crying the whole night. During the day, when I was not sleeping, I was crying. Nothing and no one, not even Jesus, cheered me up. I could hardly even eat.

My mother wanted to know why I was depressed, but I never told her. However, she did know that I was extremely depressed. She wanted to help me. Almost from the very beginning she kept trying to convince me to take Prozac. I did not want that. When she asked me why, I told her that between God and my friends at church and Samantha's, that God would bring me through this. The depression lasted a lot longer that I expected. I lost count of the times my mother tried to convince me to take Prozac. We had the same discussion every time.

After almost two and a half months, she wore me down. I called my doctor to ask him which antidepressant, if I were to take one, would be good for me. I waited two weeks for him to call me. When he finally did call, he apologized for having taken so long to call me back. He needed to research each antidepressant to see what would work best for me. After he told me the name of the medication that would be appropriate for me, he told me I should never take Prozac. One of the possible side effects of Prozac is a form of Dystonia. I appreciated all of the time, effort, energy, and research that he did for me, but I still decided to not take an antidepressant.

After four months of being depressed I had absolutely no relief. None. Between Jesus and my friends, I was no better than I was on day one of this depression. I'd had it! I told Jesus that if this is what life is going to be like with Him, I wasn't so sure I wanted a life with Jesus! Immediately I heard the Lord say to me, "Laurie, if you are willing to leave me when times get rough, how can I trust you with one of my sons?" It took me a second to get it. "Whooooooa. I'm sorry Lord. Now I get it." A day or two later, the depression lifted.

Chapter 17

About eight months after my depression lifted, Paul and Yvette became engaged for Valentine's Day. This threw me back into another very similar depression. However, there was still hope! Yvette did not have him for sure until the wedding ceremony. They set the date for that August. Paul had plenty of time to back out of the relationship with Yvette and come back to me.

I received a wedding invitation. Things did not look good for Paul and me. I was hoping against hope. I made sure I had a nice, handsome, Christian man to be my date for the wedding. The evening before the wedding, I called my friend Dave and told him I could not go to this wedding. He told me I could, and that I had to go. I listened. My date and I went to the church. Paul was going to go through with his marriage. During the ceremony, I was crying. Everyone in the church thought they were tears of joy.

When my date and I arrived at the reception, I was not doing well. Then came the first dance. I politely excused myself, went out into the hall, and began to cry. Through these tears I prayed, "Lord, if you want me to stay, you are going to have to give me the strength! I can't do this by myself!" He gave me the strength. I pretended it was a huge party and I danced most of the time. I had a ball!

After the reception, when I returned home and I was alone with just the Lord, I realized that Paul had married Yvette. It was too late for me to still marry Paul and I broke down crying.

The next morning after church services, I cried and cried. I cried over Paul for a long while afterwards. However, I learned a very important lesson. People, even though we think we want God to answer all of our prayers with a resounding "Yes", He still knows what's best for us. For a long time after the wedding, I asked God, why I couldn't have Paul. He did not answer me then, so I moved onward and forward with my life.

A few years ago, I saw Yvette at a local library. She looked terrible! There was no color in her cheeks, her face was drawn, her hair was all straggly, and she looked depressed and miserable. I asked, "How are you?" She replied, "Okay, how are you?" I answered, "I'm good. Are you guys still going to…(the name of the church they had been attending)?" The answer Yvette gave me took me aback. "No, we're not going there. We haven't gone to church since 2002."

Yvette, if you are reading this, you know who you are. If you and Paul are still married, and you are in the same situation and circumstances, I strongly urge and encourage you, for your sake, and the sake of your marriage and your children, to get back to a good, solid, Bible Believing Church. If Paul won't go, go without him. If your children will go, bring them. I saw your son was hurting, so he just might agree to go to church with you. Don't be surprised if he's waiting for your invitation, and that when you ask him, he may enthusiastically say, "Yes Mom, let's go."

Yvette, you need to be amongst believers in order to fellowship, to have people who will pray for you, love, encourage and support you through these difficult times. Don't give up hope!

Love,
Laurie

Chapter 18

A few years later, in 2001, I met Gene (not his real name) at "Heaven." It was not love at first sight. In fact, I thought, felt, and believed that Gene was not my type. We were just friends. Each week when we saw each other, we would talk even more, getting to know one another. I found Gene to be interesting and nice. He developed a fondness for me.

Gene told me that he was a Christian. I had no reason to doubt him. He went to church every week, and I could tell by our conversations that he really loved Jesus…a lot. Gene was divorced more that once. The Holy Spirit kept telling me to ask Gene if he had ever cheated on his wives. I kept telling the Holy Spirit, "No." I did not want to know the answer. Finally, the Holy Spirit stopped telling me to ask Gene.

He started coming over to my apartment almost every night after work and he would stay until about ten p.m. The relationship developed very quickly. It was as if it were a whirlwind effect. He would take me out to dinner, to Samantha's, or for a night out visiting some people. When we would return to my apartment, he would massage my feet. I loved that. One day while he was at my apartment, while I was sitting in my wheelchair, he helped me lean forward and he massaged my back. Each time that Gene would massage my feet, he would gradually go higher and higher and massage my legs as well.

I knew I was going to wait until I was married to be intimate with a man. I also knew I was entering dangerous territory. I convinced myself that I could handle this situation. Besides, Gene was a Christian and he knew God's commands. Also, Gene being the man meant that he was the head of the relationship. He would not lead either of us down the wrong path. Because of all the justifications, and me not speaking up, our relationship became intimate. But Gene loved me, and I loved Gene. I was still justifying our actions. I couldn't read the Bible too much, because if I read too much, God convicted me. I did not want to be convicted. I wanted to enjoy my relationship with Gene.

We continued going out to eat and on other special dates. Gene even brought up the subject of marriage. Nothing had been definitively decided. I never told him that I wanted to marry him, although I think he knew. But we were definitely talking about marriage. I was hopeful.

About a month later he met and started seeing another woman. He told me this because he wanted to see both of us. I yelled and screamed at him for an hour straight. Bottom line: I told Gene to take a hike.

I was so in love with Gene that it took me, with the help of God, nearly five years to get over Gene. I had so much pain and I cried a lot. I was brokenhearted. Many of my brothers and sisters in Christ prayed many prayers, and I was still hurting.

The Lord finally showed me a vision after two or three years. I was in an alleyway looking out into the street. A cab pulled up in the street, and Gene stepped out of the cab carrying my heart in his hands. Gene walked over to the alleyway, dropped my heart on the ground, and dug the heel of his boot into my heart and stomped on it. Then Gene walked back to the cab, got in and rode away. He left my heart there for the rats, mice, and all the other vermin to feed on and totally destroy.

★★

Some thoughts I have on this chapter:

1. Obey God. When God gives us a command, He's serious. Had I been obedient to God's command to not have premarital sex, I would not have been so hurt for so long. Understand that God is not looking to take away good times from us; His rules and regulations are set forth for our protection.

2. Listen to and do what The Holy Spirit tells you. If I had asked Gene if he had ever cheated on his wives, I believe he would have been honest. I could have and may have chosen not to date Gene, a decision that would have spared me much heartache and heartbreak.

3. If you are in a relationship and not married, and your boyfriend or girlfriend is pressuring you to have sex with him or her, stand your ground and say, "No!" If he or she continues to be persistent, break up with the person. If he or she really loves you, then he or she will be willing to wait until you are married.

4. Repent and learn from your mistakes. If you have already entered into sin in your relationship, repent. Repentance must come from your heart. Repentance means to turn away from your sin. Be encouraged my friend. No sin, I repeat, no sin is too big for God to forgive if you come to Him with a truly repentant heart.

Laurie S. Ornstein

★★

The pain that I experienced for nearly five years was not worth the few minutes of pleasure. Do you really think I want all of you to know this part of my life? I really, really do not want any of you to know. My prayer for you is that as you read about what I went through, you will learn from my experience so that you will not have to endure and suffer through the pain that I went through for nearly five years.

After Gene and I broke up, I repented for all the wrongs that I had committed while dating him. My heart was true and sincere when I repented. God immediately forgave me and His blood washed my sins away. Not only that, He threw my sins into the Sea of Forgetfulness for Him to never remember again. This time however, I made a true commitment to the Lord to be sexually abstinent until AFTER the wedding ceremony!

Chapter 19

Around 1997 or 1998, about a year or two after I began attending my first church, I noticed that they never really spoke about sexual purity. If they did speak about it, they basically just told us to make certain we remained sexually pure for our wedding night.

This seemed odd to me. When I was growing up, I would watch 20/20 and other similar news magazine shows. This was long before I even had any thoughts of becoming a Christian. These programs would show stories about a particular denomination, holding sexual purity "rallies." During these "rallies," The pastors would encourage the teenagers and young adults to remain pure. Most of these young people decided to save themselves for their wedding night. The ones who made this decision and commitment were given a wedding band by some of the churches. The wedding band was to be placed on their right pinkie finger as a constant reminder of the commitment they made to and with God. The ring was supposed to stay on their finger until their wedding night. The church I was attending at the time was the same denomination that I always saw in these news magazine programs. I started wondering why my church never held any of these "rallies." I began to pray that they would have a "rally."

In the fall of 2004, God answered this prayer. The head pastor announced that in November of that same year, our church was going to have a "True Love Waits" seminar. He explained that he wanted all single people; teenagers, older singles, divorced, widowed, of all ages to attend. He strongly encouraged us, possibly even expected us to attend. I believe we rose to the occasion and met his expectations.

The attendees were mostly teenagers, but there were some older people in attendance also. He had all the singles sit in the middle section of the sanctuary, right up front. There were plenty of married people there also, including some of the parents of the teenagers. There were others who came to see what this "rally" was going to entail.

The pastor spoke candidly about many of the reasons, in addition to God's command, that anyone who is not married should not enter into a sexual relationship. Two of the many reasons he gave were unintended pregnancy, and the statistics and risks of contracting sexually transmitted diseases (STD's). Not all STD's are curable. The pastor used some graphic language to explain these points. I understand that he needed to do that so that no one in his audience could misunderstand. Nevertheless, I was still embarrassed, so I continued to look only at the Pastor. This way, no one else would be embarrassed if they saw me looking at them, and I would not feel embarrassed if I saw anyone looking at me.

The Pastor even had a young man who was about twenty-four years old speak to us. He was married, and both he and his wife remained virgins until they married. He spoke about some of his own personal struggles in waiting for his wedding night. However, he told us it was well worth the wait!

At the end of this "rally", most of the singles decided to make a commitment to sexual purity. About one hundred fifty of us went up to the altar to publicly declare our commitment, which was displayed on the screen behind the Pastor. He asked the rest of the people there to pray for us while we made this commitment. It read and we declared:

My Commitment
Believing that true love waits, I make a commitment to God, myself, my family, my friends, my future mate, and my future children to a lifetime of purity including sexual abstinence from this day until the day I enter a biblical marriage relationship.

There, I had made a public declaration of a decision I had made a few years earlier.

The church did not have rings for those of us who mad this commitment, but they did have wallet cards printed with the above printed commitment. The Pastor strongly suggested that each person who made this commitment should sign a card. Thinking we would have to turn in these cards to the church, and since my handwriting was totally illegible at the time, I asked a friend of mine to sign my name. After my friend signed my name, the Pastor announced that we should keep this card with us in a place where we could see it often and be reminded of it. I have kept mine in my wallet since that night, November 12th, 2004. As a matter of fact, I just removed that card from my wallet so I could write what had been printed. As soon as I finished, I placed it back in my wallet.

There was one more thing that struck me about that night. The sanctuary was filled! When the one hundred fifty singles went to the altar, there were at least six or seven hundred people praying for everyone who had made this commitment. That was a blessing to me! To know that all the singles, including me, had been uplifted in prayer support. As if that were not enough of a blessing, the Pastor asked all of those people to continue praying for us all!

Chapter 20

Now back to the physical part of me; the part about my Dystonia and my disability.

I had wanted to get better and start walking without any assistance (except from Jesus) or any assistive devices for years. My parents, my family, and everyone who knew me and loved me wanted this for me as well. Many people prayed for this for me for years. In addition, I wanted and still want to be able to take care of myself without needing to rely on other people (except Jesus).

My father heard on a Manhattan based news radio station, a commercial for a New York City hospital. They were advertising some kind of radiation for (I believe) brain cancer treatment. In 2003, my father asked me if he could call this hospital to ask them if they had a surgery that would help me. I told him, "No." I had been through enough surgeries. I had tried enough different medications. Surely there must be a better, more natural route to good health, wholeness, and walking.

I had been going for physical and occupational therapy for many, many years. I had begun to receive (and still do) massage therapy in 1992. From 1990 until June of 2009, I had been going for Cranio-Sacral Therapy. I can hear many of you asking, "What's that?"

Since I received this therapy for nineteen years, I learned a lot about it. The way one of the first doctors explained it to me was that just like everyone has a breathing rhythm and heart rhythm, everyone also has a cranio-sacral rhythm. According to this doctor, if something is wrong with someone's cranio-sacral rhythm, it can and often does cause disease. Cranio-sacral treatments are extremely relaxing. When I was done receiving each treatment, I felt as if I had just had a massage. However, cranio-sacral treatment is not a massage. But God used Cranio-Sacral Therapy to help me tremendously during those nineteen years.

Anyway, I still could not walk, and my condition had stabilized with enough marked improvement. About a month after my father asked me about calling the hospital, he asked me again. I again said, "No." Around late July, he asked me again. This time I agreed. I figured I had nothing to lose. If I did not want surgery, I did not have to have it.

★★

My father called the hospital and spoke to the neurologist. He told my father that they don't perform any surgeries that could help me. He referred us to a neurosurgeon in the New York Metropolitan area. My father called, and it took a few weeks to get an appointment. We had to wait for an opening when the neurosurgeon would meet with me, and then the neurologist could meet with me right afterwards.

At the end of August 2003, my parents and I went to this long awaited appointment. I was excited! I had changed my mind. I was ready for any surgery that might help me. Deep down, I knew I was going to have this surgery. Yet, I still wanted to hear about it and then have time to pray about it.

First we met with the surgeon. He explained that he would place electrodes in both sides of my brain. Then he would place batteries, yes batteries, in my upper chest area. Next, he would run a wire to connect the electrodes to the batteries. He told us he would place the electrodes in one area of the brain first. About a month later, he would place electrodes on the other side of my brain and put the batteries into my chest. When we asked him what could go wrong, he said it might not work, or if it does work, it could make my speech worse. He also told us that I would need to be awake for the placement of the electrodes. He was totally booked for the month of September, so if I wanted this surgery, I would have to wait until October.

Off to the neurologist we went. He and the nurse practitioner reiterated a lot of what the surgeon had told us. They asked me almost everything about my medical history, including what medications I had tried for the Dystonia. When they saw I had tried just about everything, they told me I was a candidate for D.B.S. (deep brain stimulation) surgery. I was shown videotapes of people before and after they had D.B.S. That was the clincher. I was crying at the remarkable and dramatic changes that D.B.S., through God, had created in these people. The neurologist said they had been cured. The only drawback he told us about was that they had a woman who did have five of the brain surgeries that I had as a child, and D.B.S. did not work for her. I told them I only had three of those, and each person is an individual. Also, it depends on your attitude going into surgery, and I had a bright outlook for my future after D.B.S. The neurologist knew I was going to have the surgery. He asked me, but I was non-committal. I told both him and the nurse practitioner that I have to go home and think about it. As I was leaving his office he said to me, "The next time I see you will be in the operating room." I did not confirm or deny what he said.

I came home and spoke to my family, and a health practitioner about D.B.S. I prayed about it. A few days later, I decided it was worth a try. I called the surgeon's office and we scheduled the first surgery for October 16th. The second surgery would be on November 17th, which happened to be my 40th birthday. What a beautiful birthday present!

After I scheduled the surgeries, I told some people at my church about it. One of my girlfriends told me to call the church office and place myself on the prayer sheet in the bulletin. It was still early September. "Now?" I asked her. "Yes now." I called the church office. Many of the people came over to me to ask what was wrong. I told them nothing was wrong, that this was going to be a surgery for the good! They said they would pray for me. I received many, many cards with prayers and well wishes for these surgeries to be successful. I hung all of these cards on the wall above my dining room table so I could see them often. One day while reading my Bible, I looked up and saw all the cards. I was overwhelmed in a good way. I started crying in gratitude and appreciation for all the Christians and Jews that were represented on this wall. Then I thought about how many people had not sent me a card but were still praying for me. I had a good, long belly cry.

Then I started to become scared. The thought of being awake became overwhelming in a not so good way. I spoke to my father about this. He said that it is normal and natural for anyone who is undergoing any type of surgery to be a little scared, but not to the extent I had been explaining to him. He told me that yes, being awake during brain surgery can be scary, but to think about the fact that not many people get to stay awake and experience their own surgeries, much less their own brain surgeries. That was exactly what I needed to hear. Then I was eagerly waiting to experience these surgeries.

October 16th. The preparation for the surgery took two hours. First, my head was shaved. I don't know if I remember everything in the exact order that it occurred. The surgeon gave me some shots of something like Novacaine all over my head, and then they placed a clamp on my head. Next, I had to have a closed MRI. I never had an MRI before, but I was a trooper and this didn't bother me, until I started sliding into the machine. Then I started panicking, it became scary, dark, closed in, and real. The surgeon needed before and after pictures, and I knew that. When he saw how I was panicking, he told me to close my eyes and keep them closed the entire time until I came out of the machine. I did that, and although it was loud and noisy, I was fine. Then it was time to go up to the operating room.

That was some experience. There were a lot of people in there. They all greeted me by saying, "Hi Laurie," but they had masks on. Even though I recognized voices, I couldn't tell who was who. Then they started the surgery. I only felt pressure, not pain, when the surgeon drilled through my skull. While they operated, I had no idea what they were talking about, but it was still extremely interesting! Everything was going perfectly, and I could tell there was a sense of excitement from everyone in the room. Then, towards the end of the surgery, the surgeon asked me a question. All of a sudden I realized I could not talk. I did everything I could to muster up all the strength from everywhere in my body so I could answer him. The best I could do was come out with a tiny, little, "eeh." It wasn't even audible to them. He asked me again. This time I couldn't get any sound to come out. He asked me if I was awake and alert. The neurologist came right over, saw I was awake, and told me to follow his finger with my eyes. I did. He put two fingers in my right hand and told me to squeeze them. I did. He reported to the surgeon that I was awake and alert. Everyone's heart sunk, including mine. At that time, I had very little use of my hands, and I could not even write a whole sentence by myself. How was I going to communicate? I knew that this was a risk factor, and I was willing to take that risk, but I didn't really think it would come to pass. What would I do now?

When the surgery was completed, the surgeon let someone else sew up my head. The surgeon came to my right side and asked, "How are you?" Without a thought, the words "I'm fine" came out of my mouth. To everyone's amazement, my speech had somehow miraculously retuned. He looked at me and asked, "Where did that come from?" I thought to myself, all those prayers that people said for me must have worked. Thank you Jesus!

I had to go for another MRI, but now I knew what to do. However, hearing that loud banging noise after you've just had brain surgery was not the most pleasant experience. I was taken to the recovery room. I was fine. I just needed two Tylenol.

Before my parents left me, I told them not to worry, I would be fine. I told them a few times, because I knew how they were, and still are. The nurse told me my parents were outside, and she can only let in one at a time. I asked her to please let both of them in together. She said she could not. She brought in my mother first. Oh, the tears were streaming down her face. I said, "What are you doing? I'm fine!" We spoke about the surgery, but nothing I said seemed to comfort her. Then I started to cry. Then she stopped crying and she told me, "Stop crying, I'm fine." I stopped. Then my father came in. I don't know who was crying more, Mom or Dad. "What's wrong? I'm fine," I reassured them. We spoke, and my father was quickly relieved to see that his baby girl was fine.

The procedure for the second surgery was the same as the first. The only difference was that after the second MRI, they put me to sleep. This was done so they could place the batteries in my chest wall and tunnel the wires from the electrodes to the batteries.

I won't even tell you about the pain, or that night in the hospital. About a week later, I went back to the hospital to see the neurologist and the nurse practitioner so they could program the batteries. That was really cool. They have a computer that is a little bigger than the size of the average persons hand. Attached to this hand held device is a wire with something at the end that they place over the batteries on top of clothing. Then they push some buttons on a screen, and that programs the batteries. The batteries then send this message up to the electrodes in the brain. The brain, in turn, instead of sending the wrong signals to the muscles, now sends the correct signals. I did have some problems with the batteries, and the doctors corrected these problems. The batteries also need to be changed every three to five years.

    I began to be able to do things I could never do before. I was now able to feed myself using utensils, and pick up and put down a cup that had liquid in it. As time went on, and with a fair amount of tweaking to the batteries, and with the help of Jesus, I became better and better. Finally, after about a year and a half, I just knew, I could feel it in my bones and in my muscles that I could walk. But there was one thing that needed to be corrected first. From a very early age, my right foot was turned downward and inward. There was no way I could ever walk with my right foot in that position.

Chapter 21

I started calling some of the best hospitals in the New York Metropolitan area and making appointments to see foot surgeons. I want the reader to know, I was only going to these doctors to see if they could flatten and straighten my foot. I didn't need and didn't want their opinions on whether I would walk again. I already knew the answer.

The first doctor I went to was a real idiot. He looked at my foot and asked me why I wanted to straighten out my foot since I would never walk again. He was obviously closed minded from the get-go, so I used my get-go and left his office.

The second doctor wasn't much better. Although I will give him credit that he had a better bedside manner and appeared to be caring. He told me that he could flatten and straighten my foot so that it would be easier for me to transfer in and out of the wheelchair. However, in his professional opinion, since I had not walked in thirty-eight years, I would never walk again. If I was having this surgery in the hopes of walking again, basically, don't have it. He was blessed that my parents were in the room with me and that I did not want to embarrass them. What I wanted to say to him was,

"With all due respect doctor, I only asked you if you could straighten and flatten my foot. I don't care about your professional opinion regarding my future walking!"

These doctors did not realize that as they were talking to me, I was interviewing them! That's right, you heard me correctly, interview all prospective doctors and see who you like before you hire anyone!

The third doctor was Dr. Greisberg at Columbia Presbyterian Hospital in Manhattan. I told him why I wanted the surgery. He said, "Laurie, I don't know if you'll ever walk again, but if we don't fix your foot, you will certainly never walk again." In that instant, I knew he was the one I wanted.

He sent me for some tests and I passed with flying colors. I scheduled the surgery for June 2nd, 2005. Dr. Greisberg told me I had to be in rehab after the surgery for the entire time the cast was on, which would be between eight and twelve weeks. He wanted me to exercise at least five days a week. He told me that while the cast would be on, I could not put any weight on my right foot.

By the time I met with him for the second time, he had figured out my number. He reiterated that I was not to put any weight at all on that foot while the cast was still on it. I told him I heard him say that the first time. He told me he knew that, but that I should know that if I do put any weight on the foot, I will ruin the surgery and we will have to start all over again. My heart sunk. I had waited so long to walk that I had planned on not listening to him and walking with the cast on. Thank you Jesus that he saw that in me.

June 2nd came and I was so excited. I don't remember much of my hospital stay at all even though I was there for five days. I do remember that Dr. Greisberg came in early every morning around seven to check on me and see how I was doing. He also answered any questions I had. He even came over the weekend on both Saturday and Sunday mornings.

One of my first neurologists, Dr. Barrett, was from Columbia. The day of my surgery, while I was waiting to be admitted, my father and I called his office to let his secretary know I would be in the hospital for a few days. She said she would let him know. I hadn't seen Dr. Barrett since 1985. Saturday morning, June 4th, a tall, older, good-looking man came to the doorway. I didn't know who it was for a minute. I said, "Dr. Barrett?" He looked great, and it was so wonderful to see him again. He replied, "Laurie?" I answered, "Yes, how are you Dr, Barrett?" We had a nice talk and I was so blessed that he came to see me.

I went into the hospital on Thursday, June 2nd, and I went into rehab on Tuesday, June 7th. The physical and occupational therapists worked with me to "hop" while holding onto a walker. Then, the occupational therapist had me doing exercises to strengthen my stomach muscles.

About every two weeks I went from rehab into Manhattan to see Dr. Greisberg. He would have someone remove the cast so that he could see how my foot looked. Each time, as the swelling reduced, he would have someone put a new cast on. I couldn't believe what I saw the first time the cast was taken off, a flat, straight foot! I was crying! For some reason, my parents were not in the room when this happened. They were in the room the next time. I knew to watch their faces. They were fighting back the tears.

At about the eighth week, Dr. Greisberg told me, "In about two weeks, I want you to start taking a few steps a day with the right foot." "Uh, uh, you told me not to put any weight on the foot while the cast was still on." He said that he knew what he told me, but at ten weeks, he wants me to do that. I needed reassurance. He spent the time with me and convinced me that everything would be good.

I told the physical and occupational therapists what he said. Okay, they were fine with that. Those two weeks were quite intense for me. Whenever I was alone, I would cry, and cry, and cry. Finally, after thirty-eight years of not walking, I was going to walk again! That brought up so many emotions, mostly happy.

August 10th, 2005. The day had arrived. My whole family was there, as were some close friends, and a few of the nurses. The historic moment came. They stood me up on a walker with both feet on the floor. I could hardly move, but somehow I did. I didn't know why I couldn't move. When I did move, I noticed tears in everyone's eyes. I had been crying for two weeks. I was all cried out already, and that was fine with me. That night, I spoke to my sister Aileen on the phone. She told me that since I had not walked in so long, I did not know what to do. When they told me to move my foot, they didn't tell me how to do that.

The next day they put me on the parallel bars. People who have been walking their whole lives do not realize how much goes into taking the steps that they do. They were telling me, "Stand up straight, pick your knee up, kick your leg forward, lock your knee, hold your balance." What just hit me? Perhaps they should have met with me before the therapy session. They knew I hadn't walked in thirty-eight years.

About two weeks later I came home. The visiting nurse service sent a wonderful physical therapist to my home. I didn't know that there was even more involved with walking, including shifting ones weight from hip to hip or side to side to allow the opposite side's leg to pick up and walk.

That November, with a walker, I walked into Samantha's L'il Bit of Heaven. It was a crowded night and everyone there was thrilled!

A History Maker

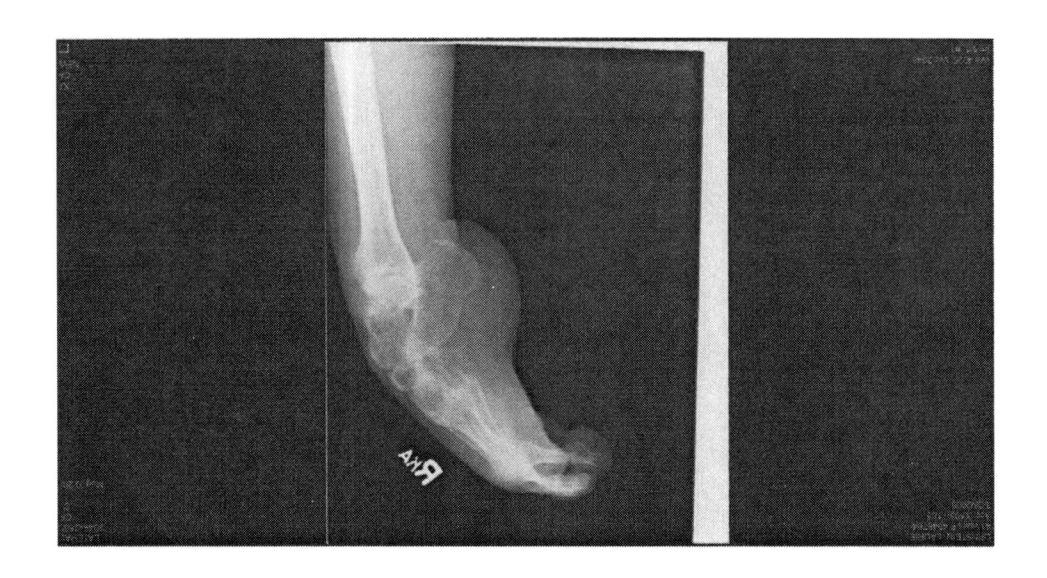

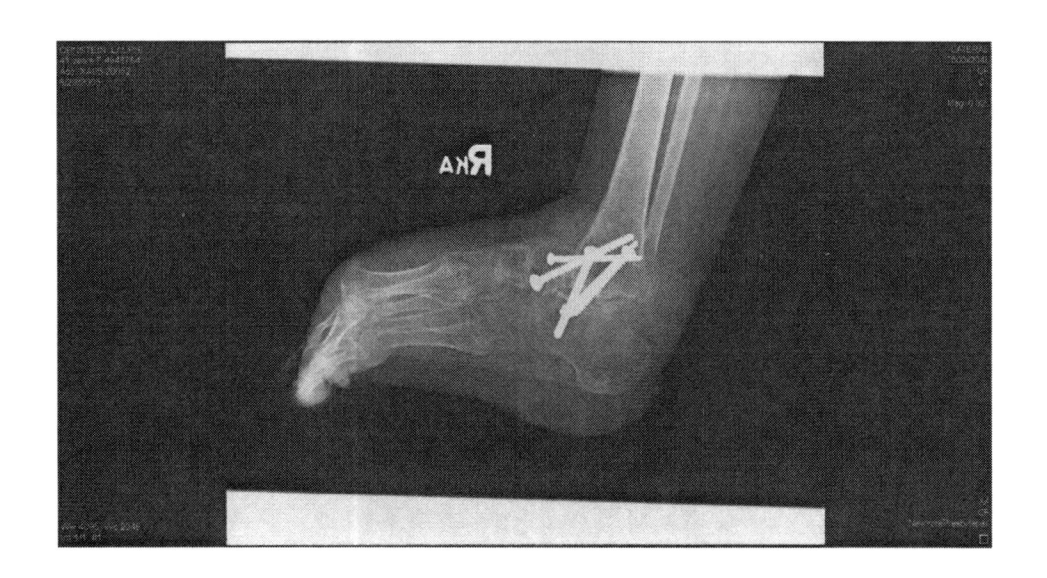

Chapter 22

For about four years I have been attending a Tuesday night Bible study/service at Samantha's L'il Bit of Heaven. Before the sermon, the pastor sings along with Praise and Worship music. To separate the tables from the walkway, Samantha put in a high wall, it's actually not that high. It's just high for me because I'm petite and when I stand against the wall, my chin just reaches above the top of the wall. Every Tuesday for almost four years now, I have "walked the wall." I park my chair in the walkway, and my friend Vinnie holds on to me and helps me to walk along the wall. He's made many suggestions and comments on how to improve my walking. I never asked Vinnie to help me, but he is the kind of person who sees a need, and immediately steps up to the plate.

Four years later I am sooooooooo close to walking without any assistance from anyone (except Jesus). Many prayers from many people of many different faiths have made a huge difference. A lot of time, effort, energy, blood, sweat, and tears, when combined have made this possible!

Chapter 23

As if you did not already know, I cannot wait to be able to walk and do everything for myself (with Jesus' help) that everyone else can do for himself or herself. I am also looking forward to finding a nice Christian man and getting married. I'd like to have children. I want to be involved in ministry, primarily sharing Jesus and His salvation and healing power with others. I want to proclaim Him to the world along with His good news and faithfulness. Let's not forget His love for all humanity. "For God so loved the world that He gave His only begotten Son that whoever believes in Him should not perish but have everlasting life.

John 3:16 NKJV

If you would like to know Jesus as your personal Lord and Savior, He's only a prayer away.

Dear Lord Jesus,
I know that I am a sinner in need of a Savior. I repent all of my sins. I ask you right now to come into my heart and into my life and be my personal Lord and Savior. Thank you for dying and shedding

your blood and giving your body. I also believe you were resurrected three days later so that I can have eternal life. Change me from the inside out and make me who you want me to be.

If you are not sure if Jesus is God and the Savior for the world, ask Him. If He's not real, He won't answer you. If He is, He will show you.

Epilogue

I will not deny that I have had an extremely difficult life. But I don't want anyone to have the impression that my life has been a living hell and all doom and gloom. Let me tell you it has not.

I have had a wonderful life and experienced many wonderful events and met lots of extraordinary people, that had I not had this disability, I would have missed out on.

I graduated from high school in 1981, Hofstra University in 1986, and Teachers' College, Columbia University (graduate school) in May 1988.

I attended camp as a child and a teenager. As a child I went to camp in Commack (Long Island) New York. A few teachers and camp counselors are still friends of mine. I had the best doctor who was and still also is my friend.

I have had three jobs since graduating from graduate school. Last year I even attended law school for three months. I wanted to go to law school when I graduated from Hofstra University, but that did not work out for me. The summer before I graduated from Hofstra, I had an internship at the Nassau County District Attorney's Office.

The two Assistant District Attorney's I was an intern for are still friends of mine twenty-four years later.

I have gone to many weddings, baptisms, birthday parties, funerals, Bar and Bas Mitzvah's....

I have met Rosalynn Carter, New York State Governor Mario Cuomo, and Senator Ted Kennedy. I also met Congressman Rick Lazio (he ran against Hillary Clinton for New York State Senator) when I was looking around Saks Fifth Avenue. He was with his wife.

As a child I went with my father to temple every week. This continued well into my adulthood. I had my Bas Mitzvah at the age of thirteen in 1976.

I have had my own apartment for over fifteen years. Being able to live independently has changed my life for the better.

Almost fifteen years ago I accepted and received Jesus into my heart and life. I repented of my sins and asked Jesus to be my personal Lord and Savior. That was the best decision I ever made.

Some people have told me I had missed out and been deprived of what people who can walk have received from life. I bought into that lie for many years until I realized all that I had done. I believe I became an overachiever so that I would not miss out on the life God has given me.

I could write a book on every subject I just listed. Most of these people, events, and experiences have been wonderful. I mentioned them to let you know my life has not been totally terrible, but has been full and wonderful.